Linux Command Lin

The Best Introduction to the Linux System for

Beginners

William Rowley

Disclaimer

While all attempts have been made to verify the information provided in this book, the author doesn't assume any responsibility for errors, omissions, or contrary interpretations of the subject matter contained within. **The information provided in this book is for educational and entertainment purposes only. The reader is responsible for his or her own actions and the author does not accept any responsibilities for any liabilities or damages, real or perceived, resulting from the use of this information.**

Contents

Book Description

This book is about the Linux command line. Many people view Linux as too complex a tool for use by novices. However, this book makes it clear and easy for novice users to understand the Linux command line. The book starts by defining what Linux is, its various distributions and as well as what it offers. The basic Linux command including the 'cat' command for viewing the contents of files on the standard output, changing of directories, and copying of files are all discussed in detail.

After reading this book, you will know how to rename files, move files from certain directories while preserving the necessary permissions, and deletion of the same file. Other file management commands which are discussed in this book include 'less', 'ls', and 'locate' commands. The 'grep' command, which is used to searching within a file, is greatly explored. Its numerous associated options are also discussed. The 'tail' command, a very important command in Linux for viewing a certain part of a file, is discussed. The 'last' command, which is useful for monitoring the login and logout behavior for users is explored in this book. The stream editor or 'Sed' command is also discussed.

This book will also guide you through configuring network settings, such as configuration of IP addresses, subnet masks, and the gateways, all via the command line. User management via the command line, such as creation and deletion of users, creation and deletion of groups, and addition and deletion of users from different groups is also discussed. In addition to these, the following topics are discussed:

- Definitions
- Basic Linux commands
- Advanced commands in Linux
- Network management
- User management
- Backup and recovery

Introduction

Linux is an open source computer operating system. However, the fact that it is an open source system doesn't mean that it is totally free; you may incur some costs using it through some distributors.

There are various distributions of Linux and you should choose the one for you based on the different features they provide. Some are better suited for personal use, while others are good for use in a more professional environments. In terms of server computers, Linux has shown the greatest use. This is attributed to the high level of security associated with this operating system. This also explains why you should learn Linux.

The version of Linux used in these server computers does not support graphics but only the command line. Graphics are seen to be too complex for novice users. If you're not good at using this command line, then you will find this difficult. This book will guide you on how to use the Linux command line.

Most Linux users call the command line "cmd" which is an abbreviated term for the same thing. The various commands associated with it are discussed in detail and in a chronological order to ensure complete understanding even for beginners. Linux is "sweet", and this book will make using it seem "very sweet" on your part.

Chapter 1: Definition

Linux is an operating system which runs primarily on server computers. Among the reasons for this is its high level of security. It is an open source operating system. When I talk of open source, most people misunderstand, thinking that mean it is totally free. In reality it means that the source code for the operating system, or OS, is available for modification to suit your own needs. However, if you are in need of support, you must pay like you would with other systems. Linux exists in various distributions, commonly referred to as Linux Distros. The main ones you are likely to find are Ubuntu, Khali, Red Hat, Fedora, Centos, Linux Mint, and several others. Each of these distributions exists in two forms, that is, the server version and desktop version.

If you have ever used a server version of any Linux distribution, you must have noted that they don't have any graphics. Once you open it, you only find a blinking cursor waiting for you to type in commands. The desktop versions of these distributions, on the other hand, does support graphics.

The reliance on the command line in the server version is the reason understanding the use of the command line is so important when using Linux. But the question is, why doesn't the server version of Linux have graphics?

We have mentioned Linux being used on server computers due to its high level of security. Any extra feature added to the OS, such as graphics, would be an advantage to hackers. This explains why Linux developers don't include them in server versions of their OS. Development of Linux started in 1991. This is when the first Linux Kernel was developed. Since then, this kernel has been advanced to improve the functionality and security of the system. Dennis Ritchie and Ken Thompson were behind the development of Unix Operating system at the AT&T's Bell Laboratories. This was back in 1969. The OS was also written in C programming language to ensure portability. It was this that led Richard Stallman to create a free and Unix-like operating system. This marks where the idea of Linux development came in.

This operating has been used in schools, businesses and other institutions. For instance, in the banking and telecommunications industries, Linux servers are widely used. The Linux command line is a very powerful tool. People who find themselves familiar with it usually see themselves as Gurus in this field and are proud of that fact.

The good thing with Linux is its flexibility. Both experts and novices find it easy to use Linux. This is due to the accessibility of the command line for experts and Graphic User Interface (GUI) for novice users. The other important thing about Linux is its enterprise versions. A good of this is the Red Hat. It is widely used in production environments. After installing it on your machine, you have to subscribe in order to get the latest updates. Without this subscription, very few features will be available. This version of Linux also offers enterprise support. In any case you can call the developers for assistance. However, after calling them for support about the non-enterprise versions, they will tell you that they do not support that version. With Linux, you can also write shell scripts which are very powerful. Linux is solely based on C programming language. This also explains power of the language itself.

The kernel is also the main part of the Linux. It is in direct touch with the computer hardware, meaning that it communicates directly with the computer hardware. It is good to note that Linux commands are case sensitive. The commands are writtne in lower case unless except in a few special cases. Otherwise all commands adhere to this rule. The rest of this book will discuss the Linux Command line.

Chapter 2: Basic Linux commands

In this section, we will explore the basic Linux commands that are necessary to get started. You can now open the terminal. Right click on the Desktop and choose 'Open Terminal'.

If you don't see this option, look for 'Applications' at the top of the window. Click on 'Applications' and go to 'Accessories'. Choose 'Open terminal' and open the text editor, that is, 'Gedit'. Just click on the search and type "text editor". Add some text of your choice to the file and save it, maybe on the desktop. I have saved my file with the name first with the following text:

I am a Linux Guru

I am enjoying reading this book

Now go to the terminal and type the following:

cat first

After pressing the enter key, the contents of the file will be

displayed in the window. To list the content contained in a

short file, this method is appropriate.

```
ubuntu@ubuntu-desktop:~/Desktop$ cat test
I am a Linux Guru
I am enjoying reading this book
ubuntu@ubuntu-desktop:~/Desktop$
```

Changing Directories

You might also want to navigate or change directories

via the terminal. To achieve this, use the command 'cd' which

stands for "change directory".

Example:

cd /home

The above command will change the working directory to the

'/home' directory. The use of forward slash (/) is to mean

relative to the root, meaning that this command will be

executed regardless of the directory that you are currently in. Now type the following command:

```
cd httpd
```

The directory will be changed to 'httpd' but relative the '/home' directory. The full working directory will be '/home/httpd'. Now type the following command:

```
cd ..
```

This command will change the working directory to the parent directory of the current directory. In our case, we will move from '/home/httpd' to the '/home' directory. Type the following command:

```
cd ~
```

This command changes the directory to the user's home directory '/home/(username)'. The "username" will be the name you have used on the computer. The symbol "~" is called the tilde and it is used in Linux to represent the user's home directory.

Copying Files

The command 'cp,' which stands for "copy files" is used for copying files. Note that the file is not deleted from its initial location and a duplicate of the same is made at the specified location. Type the following command:

cp first me

The command above will make a duplicate of the file first at the same directory but with a new name, that is 'me'. If the file 'me' exists in the directory, it will be overwritten and you will not be warned before this command is executed. Consider the command below:

cp –i first me

Notice that in the above command we have added the '–i' option. If the file 'me' exists in the directory, you will be notified before it is overwritten. Next, try the following command:

cp –i /d/file

With the above command, the file '/d/file' will be copied into the same current directory and then named 'file'. Note that we have used the '–i' option so if it already exists we will be notified before it is overwritten.

You might also need to copy all the files contained in a particular directory to another directory. This can be achieved as follows:

cp -dpr sourcedirectory destinationdirectory

All the files in the directory 'sourcedirectory' will be copied to the directory 'destinationdirectory'. Notice that we have used the option '–dpr'. This means the following:

-d – means that links will be preserved

-p – file attributes will be preserved

-r – copying will be done recursively

It is good to specify those options if needed while copying all the files from a directory, otherwise, the default settings will be applied which might produce an unwanted result.

To show the amount of space on a disk used on each of the mounted file systems, use the command 'df'.

'Less' Command

The less command is the same as the more command. The difference comes in that with this command the user can page up or down through the file. Consider the example below:

less first

The above command will display the contents of the file 'first'.

'Ln' Command

This command creates a symbolic link to a certain file. Write and run the following command:

In –s first slink

The command above will create a symbolic link named 'slink' which will link to the file 'first'. The command ls '–i first slink' will show that the two files are different and have different "inodes".

'Locate' Command

This is used for searching in the database. Run the following command:

slocate –u

A database named 'slocate' will be created. This will take some time to complete, so be patient. Before you will be able to search for a file, this command must be run first. However, on most systems, 'cron' will run this command on periodical basis. Again, run the following command:

    locate whois

This command will look for files in your system whose name contains the string "whois".

'Logout' Command

The command is used to logout the user who is currently logged into the system. Just go to the terminal and type this command:

    logout

You will then be logged out and returned to the login screen.

'Ls' Command

'Ls' stands for list. It is used for listing files in a directory. However, it comes with many options which needs to be known as well, otherwise you will become confused. If you need to list all the files in the current directory with the exception of those starting with "." then just type in the command:

ls

```
ubuntu@ubuntu-desktop:~/Desktop$ ls
me   test   test.odt
```

The figure above is the Desktop directory and it contains the files shown. Note that only the file names will be listed. You might need to show more details about the files in the directory such as the ownership permissions, their size, time and date stamp, etc. This can be achieved with the

following command:

ls –al

```
ubuntu@ubuntu-desktop:~/Desktop$ ls -al
total 28
drwxr-xr-x  2 ubuntu ubuntu 4096 2015-03-21 06:03 .
drwxr-xr-x 26 ubuntu ubuntu 4096 2015-03-21 05:59 ..
-rw-r--r--  1 ubuntu ubuntu   50 2015-03-21 06:03 me
-rw-r--r--  1 ubuntu ubuntu   50 2015-03-21 05:59 test
-rw-r--r--  1 ubuntu ubuntu 8728 2015-03-21 05:57 test.odt
ubuntu@ubuntu-desktop:~/Desktop$
```

As shown above, the command 'ls-al' is more extensive

compared to the previous command. You can use it if you

want more details about the file.

'More' Command

Send contents of a file one page at a time to the

screen. It can also work on piped output. Let us list the

contents of the file '/etc/profile' to the screen. This is an in-built

file, meaning that it comes with the operating system and it

contains the profiles for the users of the system:

more /etc/profile

```
ubuntu@ubuntu-desktop:~/Desktop$ more /etc/profile
# /etc/profile: system-wide .profile file for the Bourne shell (sh(1))
# and Bourne compatible shells (bash(1), ksh(1), ash(1), ...).

if [ -d /etc/profile.d ]; then
  for i in /etc/profile.d/*.sh; do
    if [ -r $i ]; then
      . $i
    fi
  done
  unset i
fi

if [ "$PS1" ]; then
  if [ "$BASH" ]; then
    PS1='\u@\h:\w\$ '
    if [ -f /etc/bash.bashrc ]; then
      . /etc/bash.bashrc
    fi
  else
    if [ "`id -u`" -eq 0 ]; then
      PS1='# '
    else
```

Note that the contents of the file will be displayed one page at

a time. This is because the content is too big to be displayed

on a single page. Consider the command below:

ls –al | more

The command will list all files in the directory and output will be piped through 'more'. If the output from the directory can't fit in one page, it will be listed on an additional page.

'Mv' Command

This command stands for "move" and is used for renaming or moving files. Consider the command below:

mv –i first first2

The file will be moved from 'first' to 'first2', meaning it will be renamed to 'firts2' rather than 'first'.

mv /d/first

The above command will move the file 'first' from the directory '/d' to the current working directory. Now you have seen how the 'mv' command is a powerful tool.

Now that we have been talking of working directories, what are they exactly? And how can we know in which directory they currently are? Just type the command:

```
pwd
```

After pressing the enter key, you notice that the output is a directory. This shows the directory which you are currently in. The abbreviation 'pwd' stands for "print working directory" and is used for the purpose of showing the current working directory.

'Shutdown' Command

This command is used for shutting down the system. The purpose of this command is to halt the current process and shut down the system immediately. To do this use the following code:

```
shut down –h now –.
```

The next command is used to reboot the system, meaning that it will immediately shut down and the restart the system. To do this use the command below:

shut down –r now-

'Whereis' Command

This command is used for showing the manual, source, and binary files for a command. Consider the command below:

whereis ls

This command will show the manual and binary files for the command 'ls'. To see the list of commands which have been on your system previously, use the command 'history':

```
ubuntu@ubuntu-desktop:~/Desktop$ history
    1  ls
    2  cat test
    3  cd Desktop
    4  cat test
    5  ls
    6  cat test.odt
    7  cat test
    8  copy test me
    9  cp test me
   10  less test
   11  Less test
   12  logout
   13  ls
   14  ls -al
   15  more /etc/profile
   16  pwd
   17  history
ubuntu@ubuntu-desktop:~/Desktop$
```

Above is the list of commands which have been run on my system. You can try on your system and observe the output.

'Sudo' Command

This stands for "super user do". It has the purpose of allowing a permitted user to execute commands as a "super user". This is usually defined in the 'sudo'-er's list. It has the importance of ensuring security by making sure that sensitive commands are only executed by the correct people. Another command, the 'su' command enables you to log in to the system as a super user. The purpose of 'sudo' is to borrow privileges from the super user. This explains the difference between these two commands, the 'su' and the 'sudo' commands. The 'sudo' command is normally used in commands which will change the system files, such as when updating or upgrading the OS. This shows how secure the command is compared to the 'su' command.

'Mkdir' Command

This command stands for "make directory". It creates a new directory and names its path. If this path is already in existence, an error saying that the folder cannot be created will be outputted. Consider the figure shown below:

```
ubuntu@ubuntu-desktop:/home$ sudo mkdir m
ubuntu@ubuntu-desktop:/home$ ls
m   me   ubuntu
ubuntu@ubuntu-desktop:/home$
```

I have made a directory named "m". Once I list the available directories after creating the directory, I find that it has been created. Notice that I have run the command as 'sudo'. Without this, the command won't run. This is for security purposes. Once you use the 'sudo' command for the first time, you will be prompted to provide the password for the super user to do so. It is good to note that you can only create a directory inside a folder and you must have a "write permission" on that folder. Otherwise, you will be unable to do so.

'Uname' Command

It stands for "Unix name". With this command, you can get detailed information about the operating system, kernel and the machine. Consider the figure below:

```
ubuntu@ubuntu-desktop:/home$ uname -a
Linux ubuntu-desktop 2.6.32-21-generic #32-Ubuntu SMP Fri Apr 16 08:10:02 UTC 20
10 i686 GNU/Linux
ubuntu@ubuntu-desktop:/home$
```

Information about the OS, the kernel, and the machine have been shown.

Ubuntu- the name of the kernel of the machine

SMP- the machine's node name

I686- processor configuration

GNU/Linux- the name of the operating system.

You can see how the command gives detailed information.

'Touch' Command

This command is used to create a file if and only if it does not exist. It stands for Update the access and modification times of each file to the current time. In case the file already exists, its timestamp will be changed but its contents will remain the same. It is possible to use the command to create a file in which you have a "write permission" if the file does not exist. To create a file named 'touchfile':

touch touchfile

If the file does not exist in the directory, it will then be created.

'Cal' Command

It can be used to display the month of the current date or the month of a past or advancing year.

```
ubuntu@ubuntu-desktop:/home$ cal
      March 2015
Su Mo Tu We Th Fr Sa
 1  2  3  4  5  6  7
 8  9 10 11 12 13 14
15 16 17 18 19 20 21
22 23 24 25 26 27 28
29 30 31

ubuntu@ubuntu-desktop:/home$
```

Let us show the month February for the year 1900:

```
ubuntu@ubuntu-desktop:/home$ cal 02 1900
    February 1900
Su Mo Tu We Th Fr Sa
             1  2  3
 4  5  6  7  8  9 10
11 12 13 14 15 16 17
18 19 20 21 22 23 24
25 26 27 28

ubuntu@ubuntu-desktop:/home$
```

You can also show the month of an advancing year as shown below:

```
ubuntu@ubuntu-desktop:/home$ cal 02 2100
    February 2100
Su Mo Tu We Th Fr Sa
    1  2  3  4  5  6
 7  8  9 10 11 12 13
14 15 16 17 18 19 20
21 22 23 24 25 26 27
28

ubuntu@ubuntu-desktop:/home$ █
```

We have shown the month February of the year 2100. This command is very good when it comes to determining the dates of future or previous events.

'Date' Command

Used for displaying both the current date and time on the terminal as shown below:

```
ubuntu@ubuntu-desktop:/home$ date
Sat Mar 21 09:14:06 MDT 2015
ubuntu@ubuntu-desktop:/home$
```

If the current date of your system is wrong, you can set it to the correct date and time as follows:

Date –set='21 march 2015 18:50'

In the above command, we have set both the date and the time.

Chapter 3: Advanced commands in Linux

The 'grep' Command

This command is used to search for a string or to search for a particular pattern in a file. It is available in all distros of Linux. However, if you find it uninstalled in your system, it can still be installed separately. On Debian and Ubuntu you can install it by doing the following:

sudo apt-get install grep

In Red Hat Linux, install it using this command:

sudo yum install grep

From our file 'first', let us perform 'grep' command. Remember the contents of the file:

```
ubuntu@ubuntu-desktop:~/Desktop$ cat first
I am a Linux Guru
I am enjoying reading this book
ubuntu@ubuntu-desktop:~/Desktop$
```

Let us use the 'grep' to search for the word Linux in the file first:

```
ubuntu@ubuntu-desktop:~/Desktop$ grep 'Linux' first
I am a Linux Guru
ubuntu@ubuntu-desktop:~/Desktop$
```

Notice the output, the line with the word 'Linux' and that it makes the search word red to differentiate it from the rest. However, this search is case sensitive. If we could have searched for the word 'linux', with a lower case "L", rather that Linux, then it won't be found as shown below:

```
ubuntu@ubuntu-desktop:~/Desktop$ grep 'linux' first
ubuntu@ubuntu-desktop:~/Desktop$
```

Notice also that the output is null, meaning that no word matched the search word. To make the search case insensitive, so that it won't differentiate the two words, use the '–i' option as shown below:

```
ubuntu@ubuntu-desktop:~/Desktop$ grep -i 'linux' first
I am a Linux Guru
ubuntu@ubuntu-desktop:~/Desktop$
```

The –i option has brought a greater change.

The 'grep' command can also be used to perform a multiple search, meaning that we are going to search for more than one word in the file. This is a good feature and you might need to use it someday. To use it, do the following:

```
ubuntu@ubuntu-desktop:~/Desktop$ grep -ie 'am' -e 'linux' first
I am a Linux Guru
I am enjoying reading this book
ubuntu@ubuntu-desktop:~/Desktop$
```

Notice that we have used the command:

grep –ie 'am' –e 'linux' first

Where the '–i' is for case insensitive search while '–e' specifies that it is a multiple search.

It is also possible to use the 'grep' command to do the opposite of what you have specified as shown below:

grep -iv 'linux' first

The above command should return all the lines without the word Linux once it has been run. In the specified file, that is, 'first', this should be the second line as shown below:

```
ubuntu@ubuntu-desktop:~/Desktop$ grep -iv 'linux' first
I am enjoying reading this book
ubuntu@ubuntu-desktop:~/Desktop$
```

Note the '–i' is for case insensitive search whereas the '–v' has the purpose of returning the opposite of the search criteria. The '–in' option when used with 'grep' command returns the line number. To show the line number of the sentence containing the word 'enjoying', the following command can be use:

grep –in 'enjoying' first

The output of the above command will be as follows:

```
ubuntu@ubuntu-desktop:~/Desktop$ grep -in 'enjoying' first
2:I am enjoying reading this book
ubuntu@ubuntu-desktop:~/Desktop$
```

You can also return the number of lines above the search criteria as shown below:

grep –iB1 'enjoying' first

This will return the line immediately above the line with the search criteria which is 'enjoying' as shown below:

```
ubuntu@ubuntu-desktop:~/Desktop$ grep -iB1 'enjoying' first
I am a Linux Guru
I am enjoying reading this book
ubuntu@ubuntu-desktop:~/Desktop$
```

'Tail' Command

This is a very common command in Linux. It is used to output the last part of files. The last 10 lines of the file are printed on the command window. A header is used to precede each set of outputs. A dash (-) will be displayed on the standard output if you don't specify the file name. To print the last ten lines of a file, use the following command:

tail filename

Let use print the last 10 lines of the file first.

tail first

```
ubuntu@ubuntu-desktop:~/Desktop$ tail first
I am a Linux Guru
I am enjoying reading this book
ubuntu@ubuntu-desktop:~/Desktop$
```

Notice that the file first contains only two lines. This is why the command is outputting only the two lines. Try with a file containing more than two lines and observe the output. It will only print the last ten lines of the file. Another important thing to be keen is the extension of the file. It is a '.c' file, specify that it is a '.c' file and the rest.

In my case, the file 'first' is just a normal file created using the normal text editor, so the extension is of no importance. However, the last ten lines printed on the standard output is just the default value if you don't specify the number of lines to be outputted. This value can be set to any number of lines. Consider the example shown below:

tail filename –n 120

The command above will output the last 120 lines of the file that you specify. It is easy to set the number of these lines. With this command, one can monitor live updates on his file. This means that he will be able to see any new lines which are added to the file. Consider the example shown below:

```
tail -f first | grep 24.12.162.11
```

The above can be used to monitor the file 'first' in real time. It is a combination of both the 'tail' and the 'grep' commands. This shows how different Linux commands can be combined to achieve a very useful functionality.

The 'tail' command will monitor the file 'first' in real time. The last ten lines of the file and any new lines added to it will be piped to the 'grep' command. The command 'grep' will then read the output of the files from 'tail' and print to the standard output only the lines with the address 24.12.162.11. The other lines will not be printed.

To print the last six bytes of the file 'first', use the following command:

```
tail –c6 first
```

```
ub[ntu@ubuntu-desktop:~/Desktop$ tail -c6 first
 book
ubuntu@ubuntu-desktop:~/Desktop$ █
```

The figure above shows that only the last word of the file 'first'

makes six bytes. That is why it is the only word printed on the

standard output. Now we can combine the '–c' option and the

'+' symbol. This will print from the byte that we specify.

Consider the command shown below:

tail –c+7 first

This will print all the characters from the seventh byte of the

file:

```
ubuntu@ubuntu-desktop:~/Desktop$ tail -c+7 first
 Linux Guru
I am enjoying reading this book
ubuntu@ubuntu-desktop:~/Desktop$ []
```

The figure shows that the first seven bytes of the file ends at the word Linux and that is why it prints up to this word.

To conclude with this command, consider the following options:

1. – The last "n" bytes of a file are printed. When this is preceded by a '+' symbol, the bytes to the right of byte 'n' will be printed.

2. – It prints the lines which are appended on the file as it grows. This means that it starts by outputting the last ten lines of the file to the standard output and then waits for new lines to be added to the same file. As new lines are added, they will also be printed on the standard output. This is useful for those debugging applications. Error messages will be printed to the log files.

3. – It prints the last 'n' lines of the file. If a '+' precedes this, the last from the 'nth' line will be printed on the standard output.

'Wc' Command

The 'wc' command, which stands for "wall count", is one of the Linux commands. You can use it to count the number of lines in a file. For instance, if you want to know the number of lines in a file such as 'first', do the following:

wc –l <first

```
ubuntu@ubuntu-desktop:~/Desktop$ wc -l <first
2
ubuntu@ubuntu-desktop:~/Desktop$
```

The above command shows our file has only two lines, which is true. To get both the number of lines and the name of the file, do the following:

From the above figure, the number of lines in the file is two and the file name is 'first'. Consider the command below:

wc first

The command will output the number of lines in the file, the number of words in the file and the total bytes of the file. The file name will also be shown. Note that these will be shown in the order mentioned above so don't get confused. Consider the figure below:

```
ubuntu@ubuntu-desktop:~/Desktop$ wc first
 2 11 50 first
ubuntu@ubuntu-desktop:~/Desktop$ ▮
```

From the figure above, the output of the command shows that the file has two lines, eleven words, fifty bytes, and the file name is 'first'. This is all true. These have been displayed in the order that we mentioned above; again, that's line number, word number, byte number, and file name. The above command can be can be split so that you can view the details one at a time. This is because the three figures can be confusing to some people:

wc –c filename– gives the number of bytes of the file.

wc –w filename– gives the number of words in the file.

Wc –m filename– gives the number of characters in the file.

Once you run each of the above commands, you will get the values. Of course this will assist you if you can memorize how they are arranged in the previous command. Replace the word 'filename' with the name of the file you want while running the above commands.

'Last' Command

Sometimes, you might need to see the list of logins for your system. This is good for those using Linux in production environments, especially for security purposes. Someone cannot deny having logged into the system. Just go to the command line and type in 'last'. You will be shown the users who have logged into your system, the terminal they used and

the date and time of login. If these users are still logged in,

you will be notified of this as well.

```
ubuntu@ubuntu-desktop:~/Desktop$ last
ubuntu    pts/0        :0.0          Sun Mar 22 04:26   still logged in
ubuntu    pts/0        :0.0          Sun Mar 22 12:16 - 04:26   (-7:-50)
ubuntu    tty7         :0            Sun Mar 22 12:15   still logged in
reboot    system boot  2.6.32-21-generi Sun Mar 22 12:15 - 06:23   (-5:-51)
ubuntu    pts/0        :0.0          Sat Mar 21 12:59 - down    (02:14)
ubuntu    pts/0        :0.0          Sat Mar 21 05:53 - 12:58   (07:05)
ubuntu    tty7         :0            Sat Mar 21 05:47 - down    (09:25)

wtmp begins Sat Mar 21 05:47:34 2015
ubuntu@ubuntu-desktop:~/Desktop$
```

Run the command shown below:

last -100

The above command will show the last 100 logins to your

system. The difference between the login and the logout time

is also shown.

Other options for the last command include the

following:

1. –R- this will suppress the display of the hostname.

2. –a – displays the name of the host in the last column

3. –d – this is for remote logins. Linux stores the ip address of the remote machine and then translates it into a hostname.

4. –F- full login and logout dates and times are printed.

5. –i- shows the ip address of the remote host. The ip address is in numbers and dots form.

6. –w- displays domain and full user names as outputs.

7. –x- shows the shutdown entries as well as run level changes of the system.

It is good to note that the last command searches through the file 'var/log/wtmp'. This file is responsible for storing the names of users who have logged in to the system. The command will then display the logins and logouts for users since the time this file was created, so you can always consult this file at any time. If you need to display all the users who have ever logged into the system, run the following

command:

Last | more or last | less

The command above will again search through the file

'var/log/wtmp' to find these users. Since the output might be

too much to fit in a single screen, use the 'more' or 'less'

command so that the output will display one page at a time.

```
ubuntu@ubuntu-desktop:~/Desktop$ last | more
ubuntu    pts/0        :0.0            Sun Mar 22 04:26   still logged in
ubuntu    pts/0        :0.0            Sun Mar 22 12:16 - 04:26  (-7:-50)
ubuntu    tty7         :0             Sun Mar 22 12:15   still logged in
reboot    system boot  2.6.32-21-generi Sun Mar 22 12:15 - 08:14  (-4:00)
ubuntu    pts/0        :0.0            Sat Mar 21 12:59 - down   (02:14)
ubuntu    pts/0        :0.0            Sat Mar 21 05:53 - 12:58  (07:05)
ubuntu    tty7         :0             Sat Mar 21 05:47 - down   (09:25)

wtmp begins Sat Mar 21 05:47:34 2015
ubuntu@ubuntu-desktop:~/Desktop$
```

Rather than knowing about the login and logout times for all

users, you might only be interested in knowing about a single,

particular user. With the 'last' command, this can easily be

achieved as follows:

last username

last username | less

last username | grep 'Fri Feb 24'

You might also not be interested in knowing the hostname.

This can be hidden using the '–R' option as mentioned above.

To use this option, do the following:

Last –R   -or-   last –R username

```
ubuntu@ubuntu-desktop:~/Desktop$ last -R
ubuntu     pts/0         Sun Mar 22 04:26    still logged in
ubuntu     pts/0         Sun Mar 22 12:16 - 04:26   (-7:-50)
ubuntu     tty7          Sun Mar 22 12:15    still logged in
reboot     system boot   Sun Mar 22 12:15 - 08:24   (-3:-51)
ubuntu     pts/0         Sat Mar 21 12:59 - down    (02:14)
ubuntu     pts/0         Sat Mar 21 05:53 - 12:58   (07:05)
ubuntu     tty7          Sat Mar 21 05:47 - down    (09:25)

wtmp begins Sat Mar 21 05:47:34 2015
ubuntu@ubuntu-desktop:~/Desktop$
```


The year is the default login and login time. You might be

interested in knowing these times in full. This can be done as

follows:

Last –F

```
ubuntu@ubuntu-desktop:~/Desktop$ last -F
ubuntu    pts/0         :0.0              Sun Mar 22 04:26:09 2015    still logged i
n
ubuntu    pts/0         :0.0              Sun Mar 22 12:16:59 2015 - Sun Mar 22 04:
26:05 2015  (-7:-50)
ubuntu    tty7          :0                Sun Mar 22 12:15:50 2015    still logged i
n
reboot    system boot  2.6.32-21-generi Sun Mar 22 12:15:25 2015 - Sun Mar 22 08:
28:10 2015  (-3:-47)
ubuntu    pts/0         :0.0              Sat Mar 21 12:59:01 2015 - down
              (02:14)
ubuntu    pts/0         :0.0              Sat Mar 21 05:53:37 2015 - Sat Mar 21 12:
58:53 2015  (07:05)
ubuntu    tty7          :0                Sat Mar 21 05:47:34 2015 - down
              (09:25)

wtmp begins Sat Mar 21 05:47:34 2015
ubuntu@ubuntu-desktop:~/Desktop$
```

As you can see, the time has been shown in full rather than showing the year alone. This shows how powerful the 'last' command is.

Below are a few other options for using the 'last' command. To see the reboot history of the machine since the creation of the file:

last reboot   -or-   last –x reboot

To see when the machine was last shutdown:

last –x shutdown   -or-   last –x

'SED' Command

These are common commands in Linux. 'SED' stands for "stream editor". It is used for the purpose of performing text transformations which are basic on an input stream. It functions by performing only a single pass on the text. This makes it very efficient. I have created a file called 'test' with the following text:

```
This|is|Linux
I|like|Linux
it|is|my|favorite|OS
I|will|use|in|my
computer|forever|and|ever
```

Note that I have used the vim editor. If you are not familiar with this editor, use the normal and easy to use text editor. To replace the occurrences of the word 'will' in the file with the word 'shall', do the following:

sed 's/will/shall' test

This is demonstrated in the figure shown below:

```
ubuntu@ubuntu-desktop:~/Desktop$ sed 's/will/shall/' test
I|like|Linux
it|is|my|favorite|OS
I|shall|use|in|my
computer|forever|and|ever
ubuntu@ubuntu-desktop:~/Desktop$
```

Notice that we had the occurrence of the word 'will' in the

fourth line of the file. It has then been changed to 'shall' as

shown in the figure above. To replace only the second

occurrence of the word 'is' in the file with 'are', which is in the

third line, do the following:

sed '3s/is/are/' test

The above command will only replace the second occurrence

of the word is in the file. However, this process varies in the

different Linux distros. To achieve the above with centos, then the '3' must be preceded by the letter 'g'. This 'g' stands for "global". It is good to note that the above replacement is case sensitive. If you need to make it case insensitive, do the following:

sed '2s/is/are/i' test

However, we have no uppercase 'is', so the above is just for guiding purpose. The option 'i' makes the search for the text to be replaced case insensitive.

To insert the word 'OS' after the first occurrence of the word 'Linux', run the command below:

sed 's/Linux/OS/' test

This is shown in the figure below:

```
ubuntu@ubuntu-desktop:~/Desktop$ sed 's/Linux/&OS/' test
This|is|LinuxOS
I|like|LinuxOS
it|is|my|favorite|OS
I|will|use|in|my
computer|forever|and|ever
ubuntu@ubuntu-desktop:~/Desktop$
```

If you need to insert the same word before the first occurrence

of 'Linux', then use the command shown below:

sed 's/Linux/OS&/' test

This is shown in the figure below:

```
ubuntu@ubuntu-desktop:~/Desktop$ sed 's/Linux/OS&/' test
This|is|OSLinux
I|like|OSLinux
it|is|my|favorite|OS
I|will|use|in|my
computer|forever|and|ever
ubuntu@ubuntu-desktop:~/Desktop$
```

You might also need to perform multiple 'sed'

commands simultaneously. This is easy to achieve. Suppose

that we want to replace the text 'is' and 'like' with 'are' and

'love' respectively, this can be achieved in single command as

shown below:

sed –e 's/is/are/' –e 's/like/love/' test

We have the '–e' option with the 'sed' command so as to achieve it. If you want to replace the occurrence of the word 'like' with 'love' from the second line to the end of the file, then use the following command:

sed "2,$ s/like/love/i" test

The purpose of the option '–i' is so that the search for the word 'like' is case insensitive.

You might also need to replace only the word 'is' with the word 'are' in lines with the word 'Linux' and not to replace it on the other lines. This can be achieved with the following command:

Sed "/Linux/ s/is/are/i" test

Once you run the above command, the occurrence of the word 'is' in every line with the word 'Linux' will be replaced with the word 'are'. This is very useful.

Chapter 4: Network Configuration

In Linux, it is possible and easy to configure the network settings via the command line. This includes specifying the ip address of the network, the subnet mask and the proxy server port.

You can first check whether the network interfaces are up or down. These network interfaces are defined in the file '/etc/network/interface'. You can open it on the vim editor and view its contents. To configure a particular interface via the command line, use the following command syntax:

ifconfig *interface_name ip_address* netmast *sunet_mask*.

If you want to configure the interface 'eth1', the following command can be used:

ifconfig eth1 192.168.160.1 netmask 255.255.255.0

If you need to see all of the network connections which are

currently opened on your system, use the following command:

netstat

The routing table is used to store host machines and their ip

addresses for networking purposes. It is what determines to

which host a particular data or packet is sent. To see the

contents of this table, use the command:

netstat –r

```
ubuntu@ubuntu-desktop:~/Desktop$ netstat -r
Kernel IP routing table
Destination     Gateway         Genmask         Flags   MSS Window  irtt Iface
10.0.2.0        *               255.255.255.0   U         0 0          0 eth1
link-local      *               255.255.0.0     U         0 0          0 eth1
```

You might also realize that a particular interface is down. If

you need to bring it up, use the following command:

ifup interface_name

This will definitely bring the interface up.

To see whether your machine is connected to another device you need to ping the other machine. If connected, the machine will send ICMP echo packets to your machine. If not connected, these will not be sent to your machine. Pinging the other machine can be done using its ip address as shown below:

ping 192.168.160.2

The above command will ping the machine with the above ip address.

```
ubuntu@ubuntu-desktop:~/Desktop$ ping 192.168.160.2
PING 192.168.160.2 (192.168.160.2) 56(84) bytes of data.
From 10.0.2.2 icmp_seq=1 Destination Net Unreachable
From 10.0.2.2 icmp_seq=2 Destination Net Unreachable
From 10.0.2.2 icmp_seq=3 Destination Net Unreachable
From 10.0.2.2 icmp_seq=4 Destination Net Unreachable
From 10.0.2.2 icmp_seq=5 Destination Net Unreachable
From 10.0.2.2 icmp_seq=6 Destination Net Unreachable
From 10.0.2.2 icmp_seq=7 Destination Net Unreachable
From 10.0.2.2 icmp_seq=8 Destination Net Unreachable
From 10.0.2.2 icmp_seq=9 Destination Net Unreachable
```

In my case, as shown in the figure above, the machine is unreachable since my computer is not connected to the machine with the above ip address. You will also notice that the process will continue to try and ping this machine even though it's not connected. To stop it abruptly, just press Ctrl + C and will stop instantly. Let us see what will happen after pinging the local machine itself:

ping 127.0.0.1

```
ubuntu@ubuntu-desktop:~/Desktop$ ping 127.0.0.1
^[[5~PING 127.0.0.1 (127.0.0.1) 56(84) bytes of data.
64 bytes from 127.0.0.1: icmp_seq=1 ttl=64 time=0.208 ms
64 bytes from 127.0.0.1: icmp_seq=2 ttl=64 time=0.125 ms
64 bytes from 127.0.0.1: icmp_seq=3 ttl=64 time=0.133 ms
64 bytes from 127.0.0.1: icmp_seq=4 ttl=64 time=0.144 ms
64 bytes from 127.0.0.1: icmp_seq=5 ttl=64 time=0.120 ms
64 bytes from 127.0.0.1: icmp_seq=6 ttl=64 time=0.253 ms
64 bytes from 127.0.0.1: icmp_seq=7 ttl=64 time=0.122 ms
```

As you can see from the above figure, the local host is reachable. Again, the process will continue to ping the machine, so, again, just press Ctrl + C and the process will be killed. Rather than sending packets which will never end, you can specify the number of ICMP echo packets which you need to receive as follows:

Ping –c4 127.0.0.1

This will return only four ICMP echo packets on your standard output. After that, the process will stop as shown below.

```
ubuntu@ubuntu-desktop:~/Desktop$ ping -c4 127.0.0.1
PING 127.0.0.1 (127.0.0.1) 56(84) bytes of data.
64 bytes from 127.0.0.1: icmp_seq=1 ttl=64 time=0.167 ms
64 bytes from 127.0.0.1: icmp_seq=2 ttl=64 time=0.125 ms
64 bytes from 127.0.0.1: icmp_seq=3 ttl=64 time=0.126 ms
64 bytes from 127.0.0.1: icmp_seq=4 ttl=64 time=0.164 ms

--- 127.0.0.1 ping statistics ---
4 packets transmitted, 4 received, 0% packet loss, time 3000ms
rtt min/avg/max/mdev = 0.125/0.145/0.167/0.023 ms
ubuntu@ubuntu-desktop:~/Desktop$
```

You will also notice that the ICMP echo packets will be shown on the standard output as they are sent to your machine. You might not be interested with this verbal mode. To make it silent, you can do as follows:

ping –c4 127.0.0.1 –q

```
ubuntu@ubuntu-desktop:~/Desktop$ ping -c4 127.0.0.1 -q
PING 127.0.0.1 (127.0.0.1) 56(84) bytes of data.

--- 127.0.0.1 ping statistics ---
4 packets transmitted, 4 received, 0% packet loss, time 3000ms
rtt min/avg/max/mdev = 0.125/0.167/0.196/0.029 ms
ubuntu@ubuntu-desktop:~/Desktop$ █
```

As shown in the above figure, the pinging was silent rather than displaying verbally. To make it verbalize the process when it is silent the '–v' option can be used in place of the '-q' option.

Chapter 5: User Management

In Linux, this command prompt offers a very powerful way for managing users. You can use the command line to create and delete users. These users can also be assigned certain privileges as to what they can or cannot do with the system and its files. This shows how the terminal is a powerful tool. These users can also be grouped together into a single group. Addition and deletion of these users from a group is also possible. This is what we are going to explore in this chapter.

'Group' Commands

In Linux, groups are defined in the file '/etc/group file'. This file contains the name of the group, its id and the list of users belonging to each particular group. To check the available groups in your system, run the following command:


```
$ groups
```

```
ubuntu@ubuntu-desktop:~/Desktop$ groups
ubuntu adm dialout cdrom plugdev lpadmin admin sambashare
ubuntu@ubuntu-desktop:~/Desktop$
```

From the figure above, it is very clear that my system has 8 groups. If you need to create a new group and give it the name 'group1', run the following command:

groupadd group1

It is worth noting that most Linux distros create a group for the user and give it the name they have used as the account name. Once you have created your group using the above command, it is important to verify that it has really been created. This can be done by viewing the contents of the file '/etc/group'. If you can't find the name of the group you have created then something must have gone wrong with its addition. The contents of this file can be viewed either in the command window or can be opened in the vim editor as follows:

cat /etc/group   -or-   vi /etc/group

However, if you use the second method, that is, viewing it on the vim editor, make sure that you don't alter its contents as this might result into errors. To add the group id to your group, use the '–g' option as shown below:

Groupadd –g 1300 group1id

To create a system group, use the –r option as shown below:

Groupadd –r systemgroup

We can now use the 'useradd' command which can be used for either a new user to the system or for updating the information of any available user. Let us create a new user named 'user1':

useradd -c "User" -d "/home/user1" -s "/bin/bash" –

user1

In the above command, we have used many parameters. Let us define their purpose:

1. '-c' - this will be used to designate the name of the user. It is the name to be displayed on the login window. In our case, this is "User".
2. '-d' - the path signifying the user's home directory. If you don't specify this, it will be created by default. In our command above '/home/user1' will be our user's home directory.
3. '-s' - this will establish the default login shell for the user we have created. In our case the default shell for 'user1' will be the 'bash' shell.

Other options that can be used together with the 'useradd' command include the following:

4. '-b' - specifies the base directory of the system. This is the '/home' for most Linux distros and is used for the purpose of the home directory. If we don't specify the '–d' option above while creating a new user, this is made the default home directory for the new user.

5. '-g' - this specifies the primary group name or ID. If you don't specify this option while creating a new user, a new group with a name similar to the login name is created and a group id is assigned.

   Example:

   useradd –g 200 user1

6. '-G' - this specifies other supplementary groups which the user is also a member of. A comma is used to separate the group names.

   Example:

```
useradd –g 200 –G sudo, adm user1
```

Note that in the above command, we have specified only two groups. Others can also be added and a comma is used to separate them as well.

Now that we have created a new user and assigned them a group, it is important to assign them a password. This will ensure security and that no other user will login to the system and act as them. To assign a password for the user we have created above, that is, user1, run the following command:

```
passwd user1
```

Once you run this command, you will be prompted the password and also to retype the same password. The user user1 will then use that password to login to the system. The passwd command is also associated with other options which include the following:

1. '-d' - this deletes the password associated with the specified user, meaning that this user will not be able to login to the system anymore.

    Example:

    passwd –d user1

2. '-S' – this shows all the information in the '/etc/shadow' file so as to show the user's status.

    Example:

    passwd –S user1

3. '-l' - this locks the password for a particular user's account. The user will then be able to login to the system without authentication. Other means of authentication such as SSH (secure shell) will then be used for authentication purposes.

4. -a- used to show the status of all the users of the system. It can only be combined with the –S option. Example:

passwd –S –a

Sometimes, you might need to modify some of the settings for a certain user. This is easy to do via the command line as explained below.

useradd -c "User" -d "/home/user1" -s "/bin/bash" – user1

To change both the login and the name of the above user as well as the ID, or to add him to the group admin use the following command:

usermod -l user -c "The User" -u 4000 -G adm -a user1

The –l option has the purpose of creating a new login name for the user. To delete a group, use the 'groupdel' command as shown below:

    groupdel group1

The group will be deleted, however, this will only happen if the group is a supplementary group for the users. If it is the primary group, then we need to start by first deleting the users before deleting the group.

    To delete a certain user, just run the following command:

    userdel user1

The above command will delete the user 'user1' from the system. However, if he is logged into the system at this time, you will be warned before deleting. The files and the home directory for this user will not be deleted. The 'userdel' command is also associated with the following options:

1. '-r' - all the directories and files in the home directory of the user will also be removed.

   Example:

   Userdel –r user1

2. '-f' - this option will force the account of the user to be deleted regardless of whether or not they are logged into the system. The home directory of this user will also be removed regardless of whether other users are using this directory or not.

   Example:

   userdel –f user1

Previously, we talked about the 'sudo' command (super user do). For a user to be able to execute this command, they must be added to the sudo group which is a system group. To add a user to this group, simply run the following command:

```
usermod -G sudo -a user1
```

In the above command, we have added the user 'user1' to the system group 'sudo'. This user will then be able to use the 'sudo' command. For the user to be in full administrative control of their account, they must be added the 'adm' group. This can be done as follows:

```
usermod -G sudo,adm -a user1
```

If the user wants to login to the system via the shell, the following command should be used:

```
login user1
```

They will then be prompted to enter the password and if correct, they will be able to access the system. To checks the groups of a certain user, execute the following command:

groups 'username'

Example:

groups user1

The above command will show all the groups to which the user 'user1' belongs.

Chapter 6: Backup and Recovery

In Linux, it is possible to backup your files and folders with 'tar'. The 'tar' command can also be used to recover the same files and folders in case something tragic happens. To perform the backup, the following command is used:

Sudo tar –cvpzf backupfile.tar.gz - - exclude = /mnt /

The option 'c' tells 'tar' to create and overwrite a backup file named 'backupfile'. The option 'v' is to display the command verbally, which means that the 'linux' file server will tell u what is going on during the backup process. 'p' stands for "preserving permissions". If u don't put it in your command, 'tar' will do away with the file permissions associated with each file. 'z' is for compressing the backup files to be of the correct size. 'f' gives 'tar' a filename to create and backup all this too. We use '.gz' because it is compressed by the use of 'z'. The backup will exclude the 'mnt' directory and backup the root (/) directory.

It is also possible that you may need to back up a website. The following command can be used for that purpose:

var/www

Now that you have backed up your files, it's possible that some failures may occur. This calls for the recovery of these files. This can be achieved using the 'tar' command as follows:

sudo tar –xvpzf backupfile.tar.gz –C /recovery

Below is a breakdown of the options used in the command used above.

1. 'x' - has the purpose of extracting the file
2. 'v' - verbal, meaning that you will see the progress of the recovery process.
3. 'p' - permissions will be preserved

4. 'z' - is for decompressing the file since we compressed it during the backup process. If the file was not compressed, we can do away with the 'z' option.

5. 'f' - is for specifying the file name.

6. 'C' - (uppercase) is for changing the directory. It tells 'tar' to recover the 'tar' file in a new directory called "recovery" so as not to overwrite files in the old directory.

Conclusion

Linux is an operating system for computers. It exists in various distributions such as Ubuntu, Red Hat, Fedora and Linux mint which are called Linux distros. Each of these distros comes in two versions, that is, the server and the desktop versions.

The sever versions of these distros have no graphics and supports only commands via the command line. This is to ensure a degree of security. This explains why most server computers run Linux as their OS. It also calls for the need to learn and understand the Linux commands. The command line is a very powerful tool in Linux and one can achieve everything that the Graphics users can achieve. Linux users who find themselves comfortable with these commands usually feel proud of it and they earn a great deal of respect in society.

The Linux command line supports numerous commands. These commands can be used to do everything in the system from the time of login to the time of logout or shutdown of the system.

Linux commands can be used to manage files and directories, which is the main purpose with users. Management of files in Linux includes modifying their contents, moving them to other directories, renaming them, as well as creation and deletion of the same files. These tasks can all be achieved via the command line.

Creation of directories, changing of directories, and deletion can also be achieved via the command line. This clearly depicts the power of the Linux command line. Users can also be managed via the command line. This includes adding new users to the system, adding them to particular groups and as well as deletion of the same users from either a group or the system altogether. Managing the network can be done using the command line, including configuring the network for ip addresses, subnet mask and the gateways.

www.ingramcontent.com/pod-product-compliance
Lightning Source LLC
Chambersburg PA
CBHW071029050326
40689CB00014B/3574